POETRY
now

A WORLD IN REFLECTION

Edited by

Heather Killingray

First published in Great Britain in 2000 by
POETRY NOW
Remus House,
Coltsfoot Drive,
Woodston,
Peterborough, PE2 9JX
Telephone (01733) 898101
Fax (01733) 313524

HB ISBN 0 75430 923 1
SB ISBN 0 75430 924 X

FOREWORD

Although we are a nation of poets we are accused of not reading poetry, or buying poetry books. After many years of listening to the incessant gripes of poetry publishers, I can only assume that the books they publish, in general, are books that most people do not want to read.

Poetry should not be obscure, introverted, and as cryptic as a crossword puzzle: it is the poet's duty to reach out and embrace the world.

The world owes the poet nothing and we should not be expected to dig and delve into a rambling discourse searching for some inner meaning.

The reason we write poetry (and almost all of us do) is because we want to communicate: an ideal; an idea; or a specific feeling.

Poetry is as essential in communication, as a letter; a radio; a telephone, and the main criterion for selecting the poems in this anthology is very simple: they communicate.

CONTENTS

TURNING POINT

At the crossroads
a pigeon and I
stopped to compare one another.

His ragged feet
curled and crossed
around a twig

So mountainous he seemed
among the red berries.

His black fire eyes
thrust out at me
such a jet of blame
I thought he must have been hit.
It was true, his wing
which fanned the thorns
was as jagged as a broken mirror.

He stood, grey and high
over me
glaring down.
Full of despair
I talked and proffered my hand
when suddenly a car ripped past
he burst into the sky
the twig
reverberated
crazily
and my empty hand
so high above me
seemed mountainous
among the red berries.

Rebecca Camu

WINTER IN THE NEW FOREST

Slow steam rises over frosty morning's meadow

Ice cold the air, frozen the open-spaced wilderness
Where once hung thick fog like
spectres of the
forest.

Icicles hang from topmost canopies
Where deep frozen chlorophyll shivers
Within innermost leaves
And larvae of creatures cower in the cold.
Now steam rises over frosty morning's meadow
Ice cold the air, frozen the open-spaced wilderness
Where once hung thick fog like
spectres of the
forest.

Pine cones lay strewn on forested floor
Seeds of saplings hidden beneath snowy blankets
Frozen fungi as great growths on bark of trees
Slow steam rises over frosty morning's meadow
Ice cold the air, frozen the open-spaced wilderness
Where once hung thick fog like
spectres of the
forest.

Owls too hypothermic to give a hoot
Feathers fluffed to keep in warmth
Small birds seek a seed-laden fare
Deer rake snow for grass, 'under there!'
Slow steam rises over frosty morning's meadow
Ice cold the air, frozen the open-spaced wilderness
Where once hung thick fog like
spectres of the
forest.

Then branches creak as North winds blow
Raging, swirling, unfriendliest snow
Icy blasts howl thro' the air
In such a truly Artic affair
And by morning there below
Slow steam rises over snowy morning's meadow
Ice cold the air, frozen open-spaced wilderness
Where once hung thick fog
Like spectres of the forest,
Now there lies
a shiv'ring blizzard's blanket
and a
harassing
North wind.

Martha Watson Brown

BLISS

Flat at the foot of this glacial-drifted cliff,
among its clayey boulders, gulls may see
thistles, docks, marram, broken bits of glass,
plastic bottles, ships' refuse, rusty tins, me,
quietly enjoying the soft persistent hiss
of the flat grey wrinkled sea.

Victor Jones

OUR GRANDCHILD

The time draws near and I can't wait
To hear your voice and see your face.
Events like this make life worth living
No pleasure like this for the unforgiven.

Your poor auld da, he'll be in some state
He's a big tough lad but he'll probably faint.
You can teach him how to walk the floor
And clean the formula up once more.

Then introduce him to funky smells
With feet like his he should cope quite well.
Revenge is sweet and it seems so right
For he tortured us by day and night.

Look after your mum for her love's a blessing
And when you're older no boisterous messing.
Take advantage of no one nor they of you
Be honest and straight in whatever you do.

All down the years we can watch you grow
I've a special bowl that you can learn to throw.
But perhaps you'll be into more modern things
So I'll just have to see what tomorrow brings.

GFB

HORSE ISLAND

That's Horse Island
a land of horses
where horses go to die
my uncle said

My eyes
followed his outstretched rain-soaked finger
and
peering the drizzled mist
I saw
a small humped isle

Why?
I asked

To be with their own
my uncle said

As I gazed
a grey-black shape
rode, charged, struggled
against
those wind-blown waters
to
stand free
tossing a sea-white mane, triumphantly
before vanishing on distant shore

And I, too, knew the truth . . .

Then
but
now
I wonder.

Jay Robertson

LOSING YOU

I always used to have
the authority over you,
commanding, teaching and leading you
from wrong to right,
until that day came
overnight?

You gradually gained independence,
a long-lasting process that's now hit its peak,
it's an adolescent, inaccurate motion
involving this teenage girl assessing the opposite sex.
And now you stand before me
about to leave our stable home
to meet with a so-called boyfriend?

He is no 'friend' of mine!

And then I meet your strange nice mates,
who behave like ignited matches
that together burn their happy energy
but freeze when the match is out.

Then my ladder of worry and contempt
is destroyed by the incandescent flames,
as I admire my equal
communicating, producing and performing
in front of my smoke-screen-free eyes.
Now I finally realise
that she has been
°commanded, taught and led,
and my heart is set at rest
knowing her supportive peers
are with her, through the adolescent years.

Laura Whittle (15)

FAVOURITE POETS

Shakespeare who died in the seventeenth century
Left a legacy of poems and plays.
Who could deny his pure genius?
He will live on in our hearts always.

John Masefield became a Poet Laureate -
His poems had rhythm and rhyme.
Sea Fever and *Cargoes* - two of his best,
Will be read and enjoyed through all time.

Henry Newbolt once paid great homage
To our famous kings of the sea
In his memorable poem *Admirals All* -
Hail to the bold and the free.

A most revered name is Lord Tennyson.
The Charge of The Light Brigade
Was a classic about the Crimean War -
Fine works such as this never fade.

The Owl and the Pussy Cat was also a gem
By an author named Edward Lear.
Children of all ages delight in this poem
Which is read with great joy year by year.

William Wordsworth, a Laureate and Poet Supreme -
His well-chosen lines cast a spell;
Upon Westminster Bridge and sweet *Lucy Gray* .
We all treasure and love so well.

Joyce Hemsley

UNTITLED 3

on platform one
of shawland's station
men and women move
in mist and fog,
if gods had brought
a turner back to life.
Was olga standing naked at the
window, as she always does?

yellow lights
are pulling a commuter-train
along the rails, around the bend,
and stop before the bridge,
just in front of me,
to take the ghosts away
to glasgow central
and the market place reality.

Behind 'the herald' opposite
grey hair, a pinstripe suit
and in the paper he is holding up
i read about the taliban,
but one day, he will not be there.
Perhaps the ticketman remembers him,
a name in stone, a number
in an undertaker's order book.

Fred W Kroese

SECRET GARDENS

Secret gardens are a retreat -
From the stresses of life.
The healing of an illness perhaps.
Such gardens work wonders for health.

In one's own gardens plants and flowers,
Appear to be precious jewels.
Giving colour to such beauty,
With additional healing powers.

Jehovah God must have had -
Secret gardens in mind,
And their owners too.
Thanks be to Him The Grand Creator,
And Jesus the Master workman.

Norman Mason

LEAP IN TIME

In the time
When the ocean
Was just a little stream

And my heart
Could get close to you
But now only close in our dreams

Over the years
All the changes
Of our world falls apart

When I saw you
Walk back into my life
Picked up the pieces of my broken heart

See the land
In the distance
I'll promise you it all

But the world
Every change it goes through
For you is just too small

In the time
When the ocean
Was just a little stream

Just little cracks
In the Earth's surface
Another leap in time it seems

Simon P Hewitt

BEDSIDE PROTECTION

As I lay me down to sleep,
Pain endurance I have to keep.
I wonder how the night will go,
The pain I suffer I try to cheat.

I find my soul with bedside protection,
I find a spirit footsteps in perception,
I listen to radio to try to sleep,
Tiredness creeps in, tears meet cheek.

I wake at midnight exhausted, after bed met body,
Too early the night it had to meet bed,
I tried to raise my body during night,
Head exhausted, body exhausted, I met sleep instead.

Now it's 4.55am,
Writing this, morning tea in hand,
Music, protection, 'A Closer Walk with Thee'
By 'Bar J Wranglers', a present to me . . .

All over the world there is bedside protection,
Communication from Christians everywhere,
We all protect, the ones we know,
For Jesus helps us, smile and grow.

When pain it grows, my body knows,
It hurts, and makes me wonder, but then I know,
I have to carry on to help others know . . .
That God protects all, and we all know . . .

That inside our souls and the Bible we know
There is a story that follows a road
Some may listen, some may not
But find our Lord, we all do . . .

For when you need your bedside protection
Quietly alone, your truth is told
The mask of man breaks down its barrier
Then you pray, you find you are not alone

Can you hear that dawn chorus call . . . ?
Hear the birds, you made it through the night,
Some who find themselves in another place
Can rest now, for they are protected, God called.

Smile . . .
There is only some, who finds His protection,
For only those who seek and knock . . .
Will find God's protection in their souls . . .
And this is how a newborn Christian is called . . .

(A Christian is never a perfect soul
Life can take its toll, no matter who you are . . .
But if you cry in your deepest depth
You will be protected, and hear beauty in your soul)

Josie Lawson

SHATTERED DREAMS

The stars look upon the scene,
The ending of a young girl's dream.
Lying on the riverbed,
A young man is found dead
Among the tangled web of hair.
A bullet hole, back does stare,
A child is shown his father's grave,
Then told how he must be brave,
The knife had cut through flesh to bone,
Blood had coloured red the stone,
With eyes that are blank,
She lies on the riverbank,
Still the infant within her belly,
An innocent victim of their folly.
Without hope they couldn't survive,
Shattered dreams had end their lives.

Pauline Uprichard

CANADIAN ROCKIES

The silence is deafening.
Broken only by the creaking of pine trees
as they gently sway,
weighed down by their blanket of snow.
Or the occasional cry of an eagle
tumbling and circling high overhead,
watching everything that moves below.
All around jagged peaks rise up to meet the sky
like ancient warriors.
Guardians of another age, frozen in time.
As the freezing air burns into my lungs
and bites at my face,
I am humbled by their greatness,
overwhelmed by the beauty
of this place.

Norma Tedford

DEATH OF THE BUSH

(Bushfire)

The fire spread along its path . . .
flickering fingers of fiery death,
No favourites claimed it took its fill . . .
gorging itself on every kill,
Born of an impish spark, yet goaded . . .
by the agents of lust and greed,
Flames dancing, reach t'ward the skies . . .
devouring the very land it despised.

That, which left behind in a veil of black . . .
once held shape as nature had intended,
Now lay emotionless in the shroud of death . . .
grotesquely animated from its birth,
Despatched to the very gates of *Hades* . . .
victims in the darkness of the shroud,
Their souls departed to a better life . . .
of freedom, hope and everlasting peace.

These victims of the beast from Hell . . .
ranged freely in their habitat, nature's corner,
The stench of death now fills the air . . .
of this once pristine paradise,
Did nature in her fury go awry, run amok . . .
or some fiend of human kind lose his sanity,
The mindless do not see the devastation . . .
only the shell, created by their own hand.

Fire, the fiend from Hell shows no mercy . . .
but devours all living in its path,
Death, destruction are the camp followers . . .
closely hassled by carrion of the beast,
Nature in all its glory creates for all . . .
the young and old alike to see,
If nature dies, what will be left . . .
a scorched shell and black wasteland!

Nicholas Maughan

THE QUIET MOMENTS

See them trapped in time,
My philosophers. Dead silent.
Their thoughts
Still surviving on the page.

I find them; sometimes at odd places.
Like in this dark room,
Where light was needed
In the middle of the afternoon -

Like at this school fair,
After I went for a helicopter ride.
I find them, I bring them home -
We spend hours together.

Alone, in the smallest room
Of the house. And it is like . . . a sort of paradise.
We spend hours together.
They speak of freedom to me.

They speak of . . . how man could be -
They are . . . searching; working out things. Committed
To the ideal. They have a big place in
My world. Now see me, trapped in time.

With books I love around me, and
My philosophers. Dead silent.
Their thoughts
Still surviving on the page.

We spend hours together.
And it is like . . .
And it is like . . .
A sort of paradise.

Claire-Lyse Sylvester

SHELL

Tell me what I want
Take me where I breathe
Give me what I need
Heal my blood
Simply to control my 'be'.
Without thought I walk
Do I have children?
- Roam these shadows
It's quite funny watching me isn't it?
Watch me stumble, watch me fall.
I cannot think, no brain withal.
Dried tears stained my corpse of mental
Eyes stare blank through walls
Ghost town for me
I am useless
Tell me to sleep
I know not when I'm tired
How old am I?
Remove my heart too for me
My arms are dead
The body useless with no mind.
Useless.

Lee Grace

THE JUNGLE BOOK

There's a leopard and a tiger
And a toucan here,
And the tribesmen fear what
They want to fear,
The tribe drum beats
And the tribesmen kill,
As the leopard hides
In the bushes on the hill,
The tribesmen dance
As the women cook,
This is the life
Of the Jungle Book.

Tambi Maple

THE NATURAL WORLD

Come the rain, the fall, the wind,
Rainforests continue to die,
The animals, the trees, the birds and the bees,
Take refuge in wet or dry.
Not fussy are they of the habitat,
No worries if food is wrong.
No tears, no moans, no voices or groans,
Even though the time does prolong.
Before, they ignored the weather as such,
Had they no idea before,
The harmful ways in the present day,
Of the predators that kill and roar?
Hide in the light, search in the dark,
They long for a morsel of food.
Dinner is scarce, lunch is rare,
They dwell now in maddening mood.
Birds are starving, animals too,
Bees are collapsing at feet.
Driven from homes, their holes and their domes,
They dehydrate in the heat.
Most are now gone, lost without hope,
But some return to domains.
Still it is not over, the living hover,
The memories keep on, they remain.
All of this havoc, caused by us,
We are guilty of bloodshed,
We act so sublime, but really are blind,
In our eyes, should the vision be red.

Parivash Jeelani (11)

THE NATURAL WORLD

Dear Mother Earth on whom we live, asks little in return.
'Please don't pollute my rivers, and don't let my forests burn!
Just let the air I breathe be pure, and let the seasons turn.
Pray stop the wars, let hunger cease, and let there be no fear.
Then save the seas, let nature live, for those that you hold dear.
The Natural World's a miracle no human hand could make.
A delicate and fragile thing, that thoughtlessness can break.
Be mindful of your actions, once gone I'm not replaced.
I've seen the fall of empires, of cities great and small.
I've seen so many come to power, and I can name them all.
Seen nations starve and mothers weep, with no milk at the breast.
Great terror and oppression, but also seen the best!
For humankind can take control and save this wondrous place.
The natural world can offer much, with beauty and with grace.'

Carol-Ann Hume

TAPESTRY

Our rainforests and all their beauty.
The rich tapestry of life.
Animals are one small part thread into the tapestry.
Hot forest insects leaf litter butterflies.
Jungles those who live within
Birds sing unaware cloudy skies, sun and rain
Tree canopies, sun's reflection, orange and gold.
What do we mean by biodiversity
Shelter from a storm no matter what
Artic melting, forty million species only two million found
The secret challenge go forth and multiply
This beauty God created for us all
Human nature destroying, killing and greed.
I can't deny what I believe I can't be what I'm not
The earth around us is so precious
It will never be the same again
Waterfalls the sounds beyond.
The last stitches in our tapestry.

Beaney Hall-Quibell

MILLENNIUM DAFFODILS

A bright January day
The light from golden daffodils
Thaw the winter's snow,
Their audience is now
The motor car that thunders by
For these are the hybrid doubles
Succeeding Wordsworth's wild and free.
They are the lead of a summer show
Strategically planned
To repeat the board above that says
Britain in bloom champions.

Jason Senior

DAWN OF TIME

An owl sweeps ahead
watching everything; and saying nothing,
The suckling rabbits nestle closer
secure in their innocent bliss

As vague as shadows
the little people march
through the woods
following the steps of a million years

Father Time sits high on a rock,
smiling benevolently at the fresh silent forest
keeping it still for a while,
to savour the moments of transition
from darkness to light

Mandy Holten

'PLANET-FREE-OF-HUMANS' YEAR 2000

If our world were free of humans
  to spoil, destroy, kill and maim,
Animals instead to roam around
  and rule the earth again

With no longer human ruling force
  having decidedly superior brain.
Would we have destruction
  or progress aimed purposely for gain.

This planet minus human race
  would remain unspoilt paradise,
Sea, land, trees, plants, mountains, sky
  deserve to stay as nice.

Creatures on this planet
  saved from extinction too,
Far more achieve with lesser brain
  not least the ballyhoo.

If mankind were taught a lesson
  as am sure could be done
On planet earth nations learned
  how to live in peaceful harmony as one.

Why not have us mortals
  plucked from off this planet earth
Return, once learned past fatal error of our ways
  and correct way of living first.

Audrey Williams

BEAUTY FREE FOR EVERYONE

There are many fields for miles and miles that I see,
Lambs frolic next to mothers as happy as can be.
There are cows herded together quietly grazing,
While on the long blades of grass sun's rays are blazing.

Nature at its best, beauty for everyone,
Wonder how this is achieved or how it is done?
On this spring day, it makes me glad to be alive,
Enjoy each season's changes, though I'm ninety-five.

S Mullinger

AITCH-TWO-O

The sound of raindrops beats upon my brain - Rain
I see them splashing against the window of the train -
Aitch-Two-O

I am dry inside the carriage but all around the world is wet - Rain
But to my horror it is rushing wastefully down a drain -
Aitch-Two-O

I arrive at the city station and exit out into the pouring rain - Rain
But to my horror it is rushing wastefully down a drain - Aitch-Two-O

Rain is precious water from which all life on Earth derives - Rain
Without its help none of Nature's wonders could survive -
Aitch-Two-O

I pray to God that He will keep on providing the world with
this vital H_2O - Rain
And teach us to harness it and not to let so much in waste to flow -
Aitch-Two-O

When and where rain falls let us treat it as more precious
than gold - Rain
And build modern equivalents of the aqueducts of the ancients of old -
Aitch-Two- O

Our falling rain properly conserved is of far greater worth
than money - Rain
It can transform the world's deserts into lands of milk and honey -
Aitch-Two-O

Rain, o wonderful beneficent rain, rain, rain - Rain
It can give us all a glorious future devoid of all pain -
Aitch-Two-O

Rain is the most precious jewel in Mother Nature's crown - Rain
For wisely used no land need ever again be arid, barren or brown -
Aitch-Two-O

Rain, rain, rain - Aitch-Two-O
Rain is a miracle itself created out of the cosmic mist
And without which no life on planet Earth could ever exist

Rain, rain, rain - Aitch-Two-O
It began with God combining two molecules of Gas H
with one of gas O
Which then became the liquid substance we call water that can flow

Rain, rain, rain - Aitch-Two-O,
Our life-giving Aitch-Two-O
Our most precious, unique and essential Aitch-Two-O

Precious rain, rain, rain
Precious Aitch-Two-O, Aitch-Two-O, Aitch-Two O
O please God, teach us to harness it better and not to let so much
in waste to flow.

Frank Hansford-Miller

NATURAL WORLD

Daylight comes and greets the land, both earth, air, sea and sand.
The weary planet takes a breath and waits for what may happen next.
News of famine, tears and war, so much pain, but why? What for?
A child will wake, then sit and cry, his mother and father
                                                both have died.
Another man may find this funny, with his wealth and standing
                                                and wads of money.
The 'Celestial Plan' should be revised, then rewritten and re-applied,
The working day should be the same, a little more joy and a lot less
pain.

Derick Clarke

NATURAL WORLD

I saw a bird, sitting in a tree,
I saw it and it saw me,
It sang a song for me and you,
What we had done, what we must do.
It sang about the world it knew,
When we were young, when skies were blue.
It sang of oceans, teeming fish,
Of whales and dolphins, how I wish,
That men were birds and they could fly,
Around the world, then they'd know why,
We need the forests, green and good,
To breathe the air, to give us wood,
To make the world a better place
Where man and nature can embrace.
I saw a tree but not the bird,
I listened but heard not a word.
Is it too late to hear its song?
Put right now, where we once put wrong.

A E Gilbert

WOOD TO ASHES

Endangered species dying out
Floods and cyclones, lands of drought
People suffering famine and war
Worldly troubles at the core

Oil pollution, birds' wings clogged
Rainforests diminished, all been logged
Modern new kitchens made of wood
Derelict land where trees once stood

When remaining rainforests fall to ruin
Burnt to ashes, what are we doing?
From man's mistakes made in the past
Help! Save the environment
To make it last.

R E Humphrey

LOVE IS . . .

'Love is of man's life a thing apart -
'Tis woman's whole existence.'

So wrote the poet - who was, of course,
A patronizing, condescending *man!*
So, Lord Byron, I take issue
With your sweepingly inaccurate words.

Perhaps it was true
Of the women you knew,
But today - come off it, Lord B.
Modern woman fills so many roles -
Politicians, barristers, business people,
And men act as house-husbands,
So think again, Your Lordship.

Moreover, if 'tis true that

'Love makes the world go round,'
For men and women both - then
Your view of love, Lord Byron,
Extremely limited, it was.

For love is:
Tenderness, compassion, tolerance, patience,
Understanding, forgiveness too.
Everyone's whole existence, for it
Educates, informs, feeds mind and spirit.
So, Your Lordship, though I perceive your meaning
Even on your terms, Woman would
Seem to have got it right!
Your view of love would seem to me
So superficial that I urge you
Please, to think again and
Compose a very different poem!

Maria-Christina

POEM INCOMPLETE

Will they bite?
Will they scratch?
Will they just sit there - unaffected?
Will they cry?
Will they never come near me again?
Will they run a mile - screaming?

But will they laugh and mock?
Will they think me foolish and uncool?
Or will you just say 'No?'

Andrew Jowett

A MESSAGE

This is a message especially for you
                My employer, The Empire.

Because it does not matter how much effort
I put in, how hard I try, how much loyalty
I show, how many extra hours I work,
How many times I go out of my way,
I'll seldom get more pay.

Why is it you have no respect,
Is it because I'm the opposite sex?

Danielle Gallagher

MEN!

Youngsters, middle aged, older
Generation too,
Leaving trails of destruction
Seemingly to vex you.
Kicked off shoes, part of an
Obstacle course,
Requests for more tidiness,
Issued till you're hoarse.
Perfect meals are cooked, prepared
With care and thought,
But pots and pans amassed,
Were so many bought?
Half squeezed toothpaste tubes,
Splattered mirrors, shaving foam,
Meaningless trivialities that make
A house a home.
Motor racing on the TV, football
Not to be missed
Attitudes to driving, impatience
Top of the list,
All irritating habits and I've
got plenty too,
But without my man in my life
I don't know what I'd do!

Lorraine Pigrome

COMMON GROUND

The opposite sex and I am a woman,
Are definitely not the same breed,
Despite all the science that people predict,
We're a totally different seed.

There may not be life on any other planet,
There're enough types of life on Earth,
Women, the ones with the brains and the sense,
And men should be locked up at birth.

There are one or two that I'd like to let through,
For the rest there is no earthly reason,
They're selfish, bad-tempered and want to play God,
And instincts have no mating season.

So why do we let them think they're so great,
Let them think we're a disgrace,
Women need a lesson for being so slow,
And not putting them in their place.

Unfortunately most men have a bad reputation,
And spoil it for the few,
But women can be a nightmare I know,
So the debit of credit is due.

Not much common ground will ever be found,
Each thinks the other is thick,
Women just want a man with a brain,
Or chocolate on a stick.

Amanda Giddings

THROUGH THE EYES OF LOVE

I sag a bit, but just here and there.
I have silver threads all through my hair.
My eyes get dimmer by the minute.
My memory has reached its limit!
Then you smile at me, and this I know,
That you care, and love me so.

To get up hills I just need more time,
But on the flat I can go just fine.
Shopping takes a little bit longer
Than years ago when I was younger.
Then, you smile at me, and off we go
Arm-in-arm, steady and slow.

Our shopping trolley will take the strain
Until we are safely home again.
Cups of tea as we sit together.
We just stay in in rainy weather.
You smile at me; how lucky I am
To spend my life with such a man.

When you look at me, what do you see?
Old woman, or girl I used to be?
You're handsome still, with a smile each day.
A little heavier, your hair gone grey.
I smile at you, and it gives me joy,
Inside the man, I see the boy.

Haidee Williams

CHALK AND CHEESE

Men and women, a separate breed
Each with ideas very different
One learning to live at high speed
All go, her time is soon spent

Whilst he, the man, has time to rest
A night out with the lads, bless him
She tries so hard to do her best
He feels he does, but never can win

Perhaps the two should never mix
Yet living apart would be dull and flat
Some days she gets in such a fix
A man can very soon change all that

He'll keep her busy, no time to think,
Or hanker after any other things
She'll keep him near the kitchen sink
Until she can clip his wings

His feathers may soon droop and moult
What care his mate for life?
They made a nest, they called a halt
To wooing when she became his wife

Kim McIntosh

A Life Of Your Own

In the science lab at tech, sole 'girl' among men
Chemistry, Botany and Zoology - your choice.
Yet, in the thirties, women had muted voice.
Once, your mother asked you to fetch your brother's meal
'Why me?' Your question sparked her ire
'You ought to be ashamed of yourself'
'Well I'm not!'
A mind of your own, you've certainly got.

At the church on the hill the vicar asked:
'Are you sure you're not being swept off your feet?'
It was wartime; people were rash.
The groom-to-be wouldn't have a question like that to meet
So why the bride?
A view of your own, you could never hide.

On honeymoon a little tiff marred the tune
'You're not the captain of this ship' - the words of the groom
Served not as a shot across your bows from a military man,
But to arouse a sense of your own worth; you gave it birth
When you nudged your man back on track.
You had a Will of your own. So that was that.

Portadown, County Armagh, your new in-laws' home
You tried your hand at knitting - a womanly pleasure
A bright red woolly grew on your loom.
In your blissful cocoon, you failed to measure
That Irish culture took no pleasure
In clothes that were red.
All eyes looked askance, instead.
A style of your own bloomed in your head.

And so it continues; these threads through your life
Now a widow, once a wife, always a woman in your own right.

Dee Uprichard

INVENTION

Should you try to write a sonnet
Place much emphasis upon it
And be sure it will rhyme
Making sense in every line
Whatever subject you may choose
Your imagination use
Ever seeking to discover
How best to put your story over
And be under no illusion
When you reach the end
You may come to this conclusion
Time to start again.

C Stacey

SHADOWS

To see the shadows large and small,
Watch them grow and then fall.
Look for shadows that can be found,
Making pictures all around.
Shadows of leaves as they tumble down,
And of things passing through the town.
But a lot is hidden out of sight,
Because high buildings hide the light.
The best shadows are in the morn,
They come with the early dawn,
Of a fox going back to its den,
With a rabbit or a hen.
Of the nightlife we hardly see,
As day breaks they just flee.
All is caused by the sun,
Who rises to get anything done.
There're even shadows as we sleep,
When the moon across the sky will creep.
None of these will do us harm,
It's all part of the Earth's charm.

Margaret Upson

DUSTY

The band was playing a classic tune
As she walked across the floor.
A violet light full of grace
What man could ask for more?

Do I say hello or just sit here?
Shall I ask her for a dance?
If I don't move I'll never know
If with such beauty I have a chance.

Pink lips blue eyes short blonde hair
I just held out my hand
She moved forward said hello
And danced like mist across the land

When we sat down we did not talk
I read thro' pages in my mind
I stopped at one and some one wrote
'She is yours for life, be kind.'

I took her home said goodnight
My patter a little rusty.
I turned around said 'What's your name?'
My future wife said 'Dusty.'

A F Mace

EASTER - THE DEPTHS OF EXISTENCE

What lies behind material appearance?
What's at the back of what we see?
There is an essence, a deep substance
That dwells within you or me.
Some highly developed spiritual creatures
Gaze upon their inner depths
And decipher the meaning
Of their hidden natures
Which contain all the mysteries and myths.
What lies without reflects the within,
So to find the measure of Man,
Look beneath the outer skin.
Seek the internal if you can.
There lie Spirit, Soul, Life and Being
For the individual to experience, to scan.
There lie Faith, Hope, Love and Compassion,
There it is proven all existence is One
Coming forth, arisen from the tomb of His Son.

D W Hill

SEASONS OF LOVE

We walked along the footpath on the river's edge,
When swifts did cartwheels in the summer sky.
Dog roses shook themselves from every hedge,
We touched the face of summer you and I.

We walked through leafy woodland near the town
When trees were dressed for autumn, red as fire,
The rolling fields were ready to be sown
And swallows congregated on the wire.

We walked upon the hilltop in the snow
Saw icing sugar coating on the trees
For, time and seasons never part us now
Wild winds of winter, nor a summer breeze.

And this is now my sonnet, just for you
For, time and seasons will not part us now.

Dorothy Allan

THE NIGHT

Here is the beauty of the night,
The quiet reflect on an age-old plight.
The stars abundant in their home,
I look around I am all alone.
The dark so dark, to ease the pain,
The small specks of light I see again.
And when I sleep the night is so real,
The pleasures hold me, that I feel.
Then we emerge and the calm has begun,
We walk we talk we have some fun.
I feel I can fly, when the dark takes hold,
I shiver as I feel the cold,
The night so beautiful, so relaxed,
I wonder and think of all the facts.
I am here standing all alone,
A prisoner in my own home.

Dawn Graham

SUMMER MORNING

As summer brings a hazy sky,
And birds that stir and sing their song,
I'm only glad that I can hear,
Sweet morning's summer pleasure throng,
With morning dew so wet to touch,
And spider's web of glistening weave,
Oh how still the air and fresh,
Of fragrant scent the flowers leave,
Rabbits playful white tails bob,
And weary fox to lair must go,
Ever watchful badgers play,
Before they too must hide from view,
I am content to sit and watch,
And look at Nature's morning call,
For life is short for everyone,
Even mortals one and all.

B Smedley

THAT BEACH BY THE SEA

My memories take me back sometimes
to where it all began
to that beach by the sea
where as lovers we both ran.
Just me and you running free against the wind
as fast as we both can
with the wind blowing in our hair
the air filled with your laughter.
There on that beach we just didn't care
too much about tomorrow
or being happy for ever after.
There on that beach we spelled out our names
within the wet sand within a lonely love heart.
At the time we said 'I love you'
as if we meant it with words from the heart.
There on that beach we'd talk for hours
just me and you like lovers often do,
of all those things we might like to be,
of all those places we might like to go to.
We'd tell each other our secret dreams
as we said 'I love you.'
These days the beach is empty
for me it's never felt the same.
Ever since you left and went away
the wind has blown colder
the wet sand on the shore
can't remember your name.
Now there's no sound of your laughter.
First there was your love
now this loneliness comes after.

K Lake

MUSTY

Old Musty bad news flooding in
Travel well alone at that point
Will he won't he sinner man
Allah and Stella still the same

Musty feels good too true
Single sweet female truth
Will out in a trice
Who knows where it will end

Busted broken battered soul
Lifelong habit of devotion
Married to a single white male
Musty left off looked shattered

S M Thompson

VISUAL BEAUTY

Picture the most beautiful place in the world.
Imprint it on your mind.
Now imagine you're in a room full of people
In walks this beauty.
No longer a view miles away,
But a vision of true beauty across the room
Is real is living.
We all know nothing will ever be spoken
Don't want to shatter the illusion.

People ridicule me for having this opinion.
They have told me that I'm shallow.
I can't help seeing true beauty.
It's the same as seeing a beautiful view
We don't know exactly what species lives there
Or what damage is done.
What harm is there in looking
For it's not the looking that spoils.
It's the pollution emitted today.

Hannah Shooter

TIME TO REFLECT

So many thoughts inside my head
passing gravestones along the way,
memorials of those long dead,
sun dispelling the clouds of grey.

Solemnity and utter peace,
not even the sound of a bird,
feelings that never seem to cease,
the inner voice that's always heard.

Seeing the page open today,
Book of Remembrance viewed with tears,
so many things I need to say,
thank you again for happy years.

'Though time goes on, I miss you still,
the love we shared still part of me,
the empty hours so hard to fill,
you're always in my memory.

A Odger

ODE TO MY GRANDDAUGHTER SHERIE

I have a little granddaughter
Well, not so little now,
I sel dom ever see her
And I miss her so, and how!

I'm going to see her soon
But not quite soon enough,
And give her lots of hugs
And all that kind of stuff.

I love her very dearly
It brings a tear to my eye
But I know she's very happy
So I really shouldn't cry.

It makes it very difficult
Living far away
If we lived a little closer
I could see her every day.

But it makes her very special
Going all that long long way
It's not the kind of journey
You can tackle any day.

She's my little ray of sunshine
And it makes it all worthwhile
To travel all that distance
Just to see her lovely smile.

My lovely little granddaughter
I'm sending this to you,
So that in-between my visits
You can think about me too.

Trisha Buchanan

ALL IN A DAY

Woke up in the normal way,
To a lovely sunny day.
Around the breakfast table we sat,
Not much time to chat.
At the front door a hug and kiss,
Making sure his keys he doesn't miss.
Down the drive with one last glance.
He'd ring home first chance.

Just time to gather my thoughts,
Before I leave for work.
Sit down with my cup of tea,
Turning on the TV.
Across the screen a newsflash,
There's been this terrible train crash.
Oh no! That's the train John's on,
The 6.03 to Paddington.

No answer to his mobile phone,
Surely he'd ring home.
I'm praying to God, he's come to no harm,
Finding it ever so hard to keep calm.
Feeling restless, rage, nausea, pain.
It's like Southall all over again.
Pace the floor for the umpteenth time,
Can't get through on that emergency line.

Hear a car coming up the drive,
Thank God, he's survived.
Fling open the door for him to greet,
The tears streaming down my cheeks,
Stopped in my tracks by a man in blue,
'Ever so sorry Madam. I am here to inform you . . .

I Dunwoodie

RIVER FLOW

A story of a river
And its timeless ebb and flow,
I'd like to now deliver
Well, at least, I'll have a go.

You see, this River Severn
Can be seen in many ways,
Some folk, they think it's heaven,
Others hell, the games it plays.

And those who live right next to it,
They take it as it comes,
They're grateful for their little bit,
The ducks and floating drums.

Of course, a curse or two is said
When up the banks she climbs,
To lay her wet and wandering head
Across the land sometimes.

Her flood can be so generous
To the meadows round about,
But how she makes her neighbours fuss,
And stamp and swear and shout.

'It's lovely in the summer
But the winter's such a pain,
We simply can't contain her
When she's belly-full of rain.

But there again, I tell you this
At her, we lay no blame,
And if I moved, I know I'd miss
Her of the Severn fame.'

Dave Mountjoy

SALLY

I must let the world know what you do to me
O young lady
You drive me crazy.

How can you do this from so far away?
I really don't know
And I think of you each day.

We are so far apart
Yet you've made an impression
On my lonely heart.

I think of you day and night
I think of you as you write
Leaning over your paper
My eyes widen with sheer delight!

T A Saunders

MY FIGHT

Days are getting longer
Hours are passing by
Time seems so unreal now
I feel that I could cry
I know I must be braver
And not to lose my faith
I must keep on fighting
Though at times it's like a race
Someday I'll be well again
But when I do not know
I only know I want to live
In this world
I love so.

C Spencer

LESS NEED FOR A PILL

If birds and bees were flowers,
They'd flutter in hue.
If healthy foods tasted of heaven,
Then chocolate would be good for you!

If only being a beginner didn't hurt quite *so* much.
Maybe you could see the medal first,
Then strive for the touch.

If only those around you
Could really read your mind,
Then I could just think of all that housework,
And not have to face
That never-ending grind.

If only tears didn't make you look so sad,
When all you really want is just a cry.
Then you wouldn't have to make up a reason,
Or at worst have to lie.

If the weather came from a paintbox,
It would colour my life without a chill.
Then we could all take life's ups and downs,
And have less need for a pill.

Kim Taylor

LIFE'S A BEACH

As I watch the glowing sunset
Sink into the ocean of blue
I wonder if I'll ever find
A love that's pure and true
The sand falls through my fingers
Like the time that's passing by
I've used up all my energy
I've no more time to cry
When I grow old and weary
With death upon my door
I'll close my eyes and take a breath
And float to heaven's shore
Where still I'll go on walking
Upon the golden sands
Waiting for my Lancelot
To take me by the hand.

Kerry Sherwood-Crellin

A MOTHER'S LOVE

Today I gave birth to my daughter
and how beautiful she is to me,
When I first heard her cry, her first breath of fresh air,
by her side I always shall be.

Although there is pain while in labour
all is forgotten when you first see your girl or boy
When you first hold that tiny form in your arm,
all your life her company you will enjoy.

So take heart when things are looking rough
and you find your life too hard to bear,
Just look at your child and hold them with love
and show them that you really care.

Margaret McGee

LONELINESS

I'm lonely now that you've gone
There's nothing here for me
We kissed and said goodbye,
Nurse said 'There's no more to be done.'

The garden's full of weeds,
The grass one foot high,
It doesn't interest me anymore,
You died and took my soul and all my needs.

I need to be with you,
God is cruel I'm here all alone,
I see your face, you're sitting there,
I look at my body all skin and bone,
We were always together, always a pair.

I'm going to be with you tonight if I can,
It's my life I'll do with it as I please,
I don't want to live without my man.

I'll enjoy this bottle
The tablets are on my knee,
My chair placed by the fire,
I'll put on our favourite CD.

I'm ready my dear, I'm ready to go,
Soon I'll hold your hand,
I don't feel so bad now,
I'm feeling high not low.

A bang on the door,
A bang on the window,
'Let me in' he says
It's my son Joe.

'Mum, we need you,
Kids are fretting,'
Joe was right, my darling,
It isn't time to go.

Patricia Higgins

TICK . . . TOCK

Every moment
Of each day,
In every place
Is so different
From the next.

Tick . . . tock;
The time you spend
Is gone for ever
In an instant
Remember it.

So take heed:
Never waste
The precious life
Within you.
Tick . . . tock.

Felicity Crabtree

TRADITION

An Englishman's home is his castle, they say
But the one who owns it can take it away
To build a motorway or office block
This would be the little man's lot

He could stand at his door and rave and shout
But the owner would get a court order to sling him out
A bailiff with a sledgehammer would smash down his castle door
Of his castle there'd be no more.

He may rant and rave and call the owner a dirty name
But the owner would just grin and say the court's to blame
After living in his castle for forty years
He would leave his home his eyes filled with tears.

Bert Booley

TITANIC

A spectacular event as Titanic left the quay,
Bound for America, a port she'd never see,
She was invincible, unsinkable they said,
No one ever guessed, that tragedy lay ahead.

Temperatures dropped as the sun sank low,
Wining, dining, merriment carried on below,
Families in their cabins settle for the night,
April 14th, 1912, last time Titanic saw daylight.

In the moonless sky, the chill winds bite,
A mountain of ice, was moving into sight,
'Iceberg ahead' lookouts cry to the crew,
Sounding the bell 'loud' the whistle blew.

Quartermaster Murdock received the report,
Fast, reversed the engines, steered her to port,
The vital message came seconds too late,
Ship struck the iceberg signing her fate.

A clash of ice and steel, as plating starts to tear,
Oceans of freezing water flooding everywhere,
Lifeboats quickly lowered, Captain cabled SOS,
Firing up the rockets, Titanic's in distress.

Listing to port, tilted down towards the bow,
Cries from steerage decks there's people trapped below,
Smoke stacks shutting down, engines slowly die,
Titanic rose 200 feet into the starlit sky.

A massive roar of thunder, Titanic broke in two,
Amid screams of terror, she slipped away from view,
Unnatural calm settled, over the cruel black sea,
Atlantic Ocean bed, was now Titanic's destiny.

Maria Louise Broadhurst

A GIFT FROM GOD

I pray each night,
I pray each day,
That my baby will be ok.
The time went fast
Nine months had passed
On this day
The fourth of May.

This little boy was sent to me,
Was a gift from God you see.
A time of sadness, a time of cheer
My love for him is all so clear.

Bradley Christian a gift from God
Was sent to me from skies above.

S Christian

ENLIGHTENED

I walk the cobblestone path, most now overgrown with grass
For centuries they must have felt the feet of souls with 'trepid hearts.
The path seems never ending till I can stand in front the door
Never yet have I been inside - but I can wait no more.

I placed my hand upon the wood, such dark and heavy oak
A gentle push and it creaked and groaned, but there was no going back.
I stepped on to the cold stone floor in the silent eerie darkness
The quiet wrapped itself around me, as back against the door I pressed.

My eyes grew used to the dim interior and I saw beauty spread
before me.
I sensed a gentle calming peace and the fear dissolved within me.
I walked forward with exhilaration uplifted by what I saw
The majesty of this awesome place had me hungrily absorbing it all.

My eyes searched every corner, I felt dwarfed by the space
From the great raftered ceiling, to pews all neatly in their place.
Golden-winged angels were everywhere, brass plaques adorned
the walls.
A rainbow of colours shone from the windows like a thousand
cascading waterfalls.

I was drawn toward the altar cross gleaming like shimmering seas,
A power that was new to me, compelled me to my knees.
I felt so small in this heavenly place and asked forgiveness for my sins
No longer alone in this mighty chasm, I felt a presence here within.

The bronze figure of Jesus looked down but I felt no need to hide
Gentle eyes conveyed his spirit to me and I felt cleansed inside.
I stood refreshed and light-hearted, a burden lifted and much more,
One last glance at the graceful statue and reluctantly I made my way to
the door.

Once outside I felt strangely at peace and I knew I would return
The house of God holds no fear for me now, and I have so much
to learn.
I retraced my steps down the cobblestone path, through the lychgate
and beyond
I turned to take another look at the place I now know I belong.

Maureen Gard

DYING TO BE FAMOUS

My epitaph I think should be kept short
with words chosen after a lot of thought.

The few words upon my glittering stone
shouldn't reflect that I'm here alone.

The lasting memory left of me should be
of that fun-loving person from number 33.

A simple but humorous touch I declare
and no words of sorrow which I despair.

A touching tribute which reflects just me,
Deb Neale, a very big Anchor Books devotee.

Then, if I die rich a statue by my grave
to reflect the loyal way in which I behaved.

Nothing at all too dull, boring or bland,
perhaps a scaled model of my right hand?

Placed in my hand there could be a quill
reflecting inspiration, and my writing skill.

Another thought, a bright blue granite plinth
gracefully scalloped and shaped like a hyacinth.

Although writing for years I've never had my name
associated at all, with either money or fame.

So, I shall be placed deep in the ground
with no flowers and not one mourner around.

My grave will have no beautiful statue there
and like my coffin, it will be cheap and bare.

What then will be upon my stone I hear you say,
probably only the year in which I passed away.

Yet how different this story could soon be,
if only Anchor Books had some more of my poetry.

They could see and publish my work as it is
then pay me loads for being a poetry whizz.

Debra Neale

SOFT SUMMER'S DAY

Into the blushing fields of May
Our love in bloom
In her my Chelsea show of June
The so beautiful orchard
She kept hidden from display

But I found it on that very special day
Feeding the beauty as we explored
The light of her that so became
An open door, to overflow
Into the blushing fields of May

And our love
Was in perfume
On that soft summer's day.

Denis Noel Manley

DILEMMA

If you asked me
Would I leave them
To go to you,
What would I say?
What would I do?
Duty or love,
Which to choose?
Neither to win,
Both to lose.
Have I the courage
To walk away?
Or would the ties of habit
Make me stay?
So don't ask me
Would I leave them
To go to you,
Because I don't know
What I'd say,
I don't know
What I'd do.

Joyce Brown

GUIDELINES

Do we need failure to appreciate success
And unrest to know the meaning of content,
Must we first learn to say no to understand yes
And first handle the straight to conquer the bent.

Before we feel joy must we experience pain
And walk through the dark to emerge into the light.
Must we suffer great loss to appreciate gain
And firstly do wrong to know what is right.

Do we have to be penniless to be careful with money,
To reach great heights must we first sink down low.
Eat of life's bitter poison so we can taste the honey
And take a wrong turning to find the right way to go.

Must we first be foolish in order to grow wise,
To enter Heaven must we fight our way through Hell
And to recognise the truth be familiar with lies
And examine those around us to know ourselves well.

Maryrose Walmsley

A WINTER'S KISS

With haunting whispers
Mother Nature calls
Upon the wind;
Winter's on her way.

You can feel her cold bite
In the air
Folding around you
Like a blanket.

Leaves fall from the trees,
Flowers wither,
Petals fall,
When touched by her icy kiss;
As if awaiting
Winter's sleep.

J Hood

OUR TILLY

Our Tilly is my pride and joy
For her I've waited long.
No, she's not a baby
Or a doggie with a pong!

She greets me every morning.
her silence she will hide.
Her spelling is word perfect,
In her I can confide.

I like to play a game with her
And she will join in too.
Just to see which one of us
Is first to spot a clue.

Our brains are matched and ready to go
But maybe I am faster.
She has to take a message from me
Or it could be a disaster.

Yes. She is most suitable
Clever and much brighter.
I wouldn't swap her for the world
Cos she's Tilly my typewriter.

Dilly Parry

VALENTINE . . . ?

Tell me why I should be *your* Valentine,
'Cos, thus far, I ain't had too many bids.
Just tell me *how* I could make *your* sun shine,
Being married awhile, with grown-up kids.
With a hefty mortgage around my neck,
It's being said, I'm a middle-aged wreck:
Like a soured grape on a withered vine;
Giving vinegar, not a vintage wine.
Aw, come on now, don't be a masochist -
I've not a mind to deepen your sorrow.
And that's it, all said, if you get my gist . . .
Or is it some cash you want to borrow . . .?
Oh! deary me, you're a silly old fool,
No wonder our marriage is somewhat cool!

S Wilfred Croxtall

ON SOME FERMANAGH SHORE

Soft rain falls over the Fermanagh fields
And through the misty green the Lough lies low
I watch the shimmering water as a shadow steals
Across this magic Erne I love and know.

For at the tiny church where you now lie
The beeches gently shade your recent bed
The only sound the winds that softly sigh
And toss the burnished leaves on which I tread

But how can I be sad when you have gone
Beyond your pain and suffering? To that land
Where angels stand in wait to bid you come
Their arms outstretched to take you by the hand.

And if for one brief moment you could turn
To see the life you've lived, be glad and smile
For all you've touched have lived and loved and learned
A million precious moments lost in time.

Then turn again to face that glorious light
And be not sad for us, here, left behind
With memories, warming dreams both day and night
As we remember you, so good and kind.

For you cannot be ever far away
When every time I look upon Erne's shore
And hear its waters lapping day by day
The echo of your voice for evermore.

Lynda E Tavakoli

A DOG'S LIFE?

I am a dog therefore I pee
Respecting neither leg nor tree
This reflex action I perform
Whereby you find your leg goes warm
I'm doing this to mark my ground
And warn off any other hound
I whine, I yap and bark a lot
Seeing those cats off like a shot

I'm really not affectionate
Companion rather than a pet
I have inanimate objects
With which I have casual sex
Occasionally I fetch a ball
And sometimes come if you should call
Yet unashamed when I see fit
To find manure and roll in it

Theoretically, my colour's white
But actually that's not quite right
Suppose you'd call my colour dun
To reach this shade's a lot of fun
Well certainly it is for me!
Master of my own destiny
And one thing you can guarantee
I am a dog therefore I pee.

John Smurthwaite

EVERYONE IS GONE

No waking in the morning,
With someone by my side.
My loneliness surrounds me,
There's nowhere I can hide.

The pain and sorrow hurts me,
Deep down in my soul.
The emptiness within me,
Is like a gaping hole.

No-one I can turn to,
Nowhere I can run.
My life is dark and empty,
Cos you took away my sun.

All is quiet around me,
It's dark and empty here.
The noise of children playing,
Still sounds so very clear.

My children when I see them,
Make me feel alive
And when they all go home again,
I sit and cry inside.

The minutes tick by slowly,
Every night and every day.
It's been like this for five years,
Since my husband passed away.

Dawn & Marie Cocksedge

DISORIENTATED MIND

An aura of congestion prevails
Within my ever-confused mind
Past, present and future mingle
To obscure what I need to find.

Flashes of a five year-old child
Mixed up with a bride of sixteen
All tangle with a web of worry
About places I've not yet been.

I walk a path arm in arm
With daughter's older than me
If I could only clarify each era
Then my mind would be set free.

I could visit each separate era
Returning always to the present time
So my mind would be clearer
And sanity again would be mine.

Irene Hanson

TO THE MOON

Oh, changeful shape who rules by night,
Albeit with a borrowed light!
  Who art pale and wan by light of day
  And canst not shed a single ray.

Thou knowest thou fits this likeness ill,
Nevertheless, I love thee still:
  Though much thou seest when crossing the sky,
  Dost gossip not, nor tell a lie.

HJGB

FREEDOM

When I was young so long ago
I rose up with the lark
And when free from school
I played across the parks

The air so sweet a joy to breathe
And summer's days so long
All the birds their story told
And filled the air with song

Wild flowers there to view
Unsprayed with poison yet
The cobwebs glisten with the dew
The grass with it is wet

The hedge alive with the hum of bees
The butterfly on wing
Reeds in the osier bed
Rustled by summer breeze

All these things of summer
My senses sent to tease
The fisherman on the river bank
With lunch box by his side

These freedoms were English
Plain for all to see
Uncluttered by rules made by fools
Those from the EEC.

B D Vissian

ON HOLIDAY

Tunisia, Tunisia
Shifting, drifting sand
One dinar, one dinar?
The cry of the land.
On safari we went
In search of adventures
Perched on a camel
Clutching our dentures!
In the desert the night we spent
No! not in a crummy tent
But a luxurious hotel
With thermal pool
I may be old
But I'm nobody's fool!
More travelling next day
This time by train
Through mountains and gorges
Amidst rocky terrain
Then back to 'Souse'
For a well-earned rest
I know, you know, what's coming next!
One dinar, one dinar?
The cry of the land
Waiting, waiting with open hand.

Sandra Lowe

FRIENDS

We may have lots of friends,
Loving and really true,
But when the crunch comes
They narrow down to just a few.
These are simply wonderful
They help you in every way;
Money, gifts and sympathy
You hope you can repay.
Friends may be your neighbours
Or people you hardly know,
But they appear in an emergency,
To ease the tears that flow.
They don't ask for any thanks
Or think you're in their debt.
When all the trauma is over
They disappear, but you don't forget.
That's how our life should be,
Helping others as they help us.
Not asking for any reward,
Avoiding all the fuss.
So *friend* is such a heartfelt word
It should be used much more.
It's been around for centuries
And not just at your door.
Friends are always there for you
Whenever your need is great.
They never turn the other cheek,
And they are rarely too late.

Ray Kirby

DEFYING THE FALL

Bravely the small stone cottage clings
Weather-beaten the cliff face agonises all.
Centuries of crashing seas etch their massive toll
Long gone her coastal residents
Fenced off, standing proud each wall
As though every slate and stone
In defiance against the elements
Rebuke the underlying weakened core.
Old men 'locals' as if their respect to show
Trudge the coastal path, staring
Almost in disbelief remembering when
She stood with children around her playing
Many chains from the cliff face then.
Questioning, 'Was it really so long ago?'
No coastal defences to protect her.
Her future little chance to grow.
How long for this brave old lady
Before nature's dice takes its final throw.

Roger S Foster

ENTER THE MILLENNIUM

One man relaxes in the cabin
of a luxury yacht;
One man crouches under a wall
(it's all he's got);
One man glances from a porthole
at the sun going down;
One man watches a rat hole
with a serious frown;
The sun descended, one man
eats his fill;
The waiting ended, one man
makes a kill.

R N Taber

My Mother's Grave

The leaves have fallen
on my mother's grave
the cross battered by the wind
who's greedy arms
ravaged the tall chrysanthemums.

There I stood again
embracing the sullen darkness
not a sound
other than nature's voice
on the pensive night of All Souls.

I cannot speak to you
you cannot laugh with me
we share our tears no longer
nor the touch of hand and mind
our power vanished, your spirit gone.

I'm left alone and sad
your gentle, guiding voice,
your smile now etched in sleep.
I want to move the earth
and see your face, once more
and lie beside you, facing Heaven.

Marion Roberts

THE BIRD IN THE TREE

There's a bird in the tree and he's looking at me
As I'm strolling along through the town
He's chirping away on this warm sunny day
While he busily preens his soft down.

He looks like a swallow is he starting to follow?
Imagination is playing with me
As he circles around making high squawking sounds.
His tactics I'm starting to see.

He flies tree to tree, yes he's following me
It's making me a nervous wreck
For he might fly so low on my head he could go
And give it a right vicious peck.

Now he's over my head and I'm starting to dread
Oh, I hope that his aim isn't true!
As he lets go his packet just misses my jacket
Lands just inches away from my shoe.

Phew! That's a relief but my respite was brief
As I laughed and looked up to the sky
I'm sure he did smile as another hot pile
Landed right on the ball of my eye.

Now I know it's absurd to be miffed by a bird
But the next time I'm telling you that
If I look in the sky he won't get my eye
I'll wear glasses and a broad hat.

Ray Moore

THE DAWN IS LIKE A LADY

The dawn is like a lady,
Arriving at the Ball,
Where everything is shady;
Entering the hall,
And when she appears in gorgeous light,
In rays of finest gold;
Banishing all fears of night,
Her story can be told.
'Woman's (presentation) . . .'
The poet reputedly said;
'The most wondrous in all creation;'
Starting from her head!
A dress of blue exquisitely sheer!
Radiant in the light;
Reflection of a chandelier;
Defying all in sight!
A look that would astonish;
All who flee in dread;
Whose hearts should would admonish,
'I'm not easily led!'

A face - just like the Peloponn;'
That juts out in the sea,
The prow that Helen stood upon,
Beside her lover free;
Eyes the deepest azure blue,
Set within a cloud,
Making her so sure and true,
Each time she laughs out loud!
Skin like daubs of cotton,
Tinged with pink or beige,
Depending on reflection,
Each cloud that joins the siege;
And should the music soften,
Pensive through the throng,

All around her beckon,
Attentive to her song;
'Stay you wanton paramours!
Endure this break of day;'
Dazzled by her - no-one implores!
They all just melt away . . .

Tom Ritchie

UNTITLED

Another year goes by
And yet we still
Shed tears
For this century
We still see big disasters
Fear and famine
The Piper Alfa disaster
Train crashes
London underground bombings
Murders mystery diseases
Misery many untold sufferings
The computer doesn't fix all
These wrongs
It's up to us
Save money
And invent
And be there when another hurts
Children in poverty
A population awaiting
Operations
Not fuss about
Whose religion's
Right, the best
The biggest
What politics by a party
Is better than the rest
Then put up a glorified test
To say what party's best
This money on parties
Could be better spent

The Lord forgave
Us we should
Forgive and give to each
A helping hand
A vote on what we do
Not who does it.

J Dunkley

INSPIRATION LEADS TO ASPIRATION

How you can fly in an infinite sky
Allowing your heart to cry
Cry for light that shines ever bright
And feels the need to smile,
Life is to discover who you are

So dive deep within yourself evermore
And discover who you are
You are the image of God himself
Claim him as your very own self

To be inspired by nature's beautiful gifts
Is a secret of divine beauty
The sky, the moon, the sea blue and vast
Mirrors perfection in nature
All these gifts are given free
By our beloved God heaven soul

Either to destroy or to nourish the soul
You have the free will to choose

A home needs to be filled with love
A love that goes beyond boundaries
A selfless love that is inspired by God's will

Barbara Vinyard

I'LL NEVER LOSE THE TRAIL

A feeling of excitement is in the air,
I'm off hunting but I know not where,
First I go to the village green,
A splendid sight, the best I've seen.
Restless hounds and horses gently milling,
The feeling inside me is oh so thrilling,
Ears pricked for the sound of the horn,
This marks the day I'm glad I was born,
Off I go to pick up the scent,
Is this the way the quarry went?
Tally Ho! One of the huntsmen shouts,
The fox has been sighted he's here abouts,
Racing along on frost-hardened ground,
Hooves and feet pounding, a wonderful sound.
This way, through the golden bracken,
Never letting my pace slacken.
That way, through the hedge of bramble,
Up the bank I hastily scramble.
Down again on the other side,
Nose to the ground panning wide.
Across the stream through the wood,
Come on you lot, this should be good.
Can you hear my brothers bay?
This has been a special day.
Please keep our traditions don't let them lie,
You simply cannot let me die.
Passing down through so many years,
Surely you understand my inner fears.
I know that my nose won't ever fail.
Because I'm a hound and I'll never lose the trail.

Ruth Robinson

A SERENITY OF BEING

Many things can bring tranquillity to the soul,
Learning to meditate and let go of all negative emotions.
Hearing the joyous innocent sound of children's laughter.
Appreciating the fiery glory of a red sunset.
The arrival of spring painting the landscape in fresh green.
Massed bluebells in flower and the beauty they evoke.
People have different ways of achieving a serenity of being.

Keith Davies

DOT.COM

I have a terrifying vision of this giant spider's web
Enveloping and tightening round the world
And there we are all paralysed and brain-dead at the box
Unaware of crouching menace on the prowl.

Its beady eyes are watching as we move towards our doom
Fast drawn where gape its ever-open jaws
And we're all rushing nearer there in great anticipation
Of the wealth it stores within its greedy heart.

As more and more web victims stretch the coils beyond endurance,
The overloaded strands out of control
Will hurtle down a black hole with the dot.com of destruction
So the last words sent to cyberspace will be:-

World *with* an end, Amen.

Paddy Jupp

SKY

When seeking peace
I cast my eye
Often to the open sky
Where I can see,
Endlessly,
Scenes of sweet serenity.

The purest hues,
Rich reds, deep blues,
Cloudscapes and shapes all softly soothe
The mind that drifts and softly shifts
In timely metamorphosis;

And even in the dark of night,
When hues are jaded without light,
The moon and stars take their invite
To stir within the heart delight;

And so it is, uncommonly,
A joy brought so consistently
That I seek my tranquillity
In the beauty of its pageantry.

Timothy C Jefferies

AQUATANIA

Beneath the seas lie secret lands
Hidden valleys, endless sands
Cliffs of coral and mountain peaks
Dark depths where the great whale speaks
And in Poseidon's watery realm
Lie ships with no-one at the helm
Galleons which in days of old
Bore rich cargoes of Inca gold.

But wrecked by storm they 'ere have lain
With plunder from the Spanish Main
And currents draw a silent knell
From each vessel's ancient bell
Whilst clouds of rainbow coloured fry
Dance where rusted cannon lie.

Robert E Fraser

MY MAN

You gave me such hopes and dreams for our future
You gave me a ring and I wore it with pride
I loved you, I treasured you, I miss you
I know you don't mean to, but you hurt me so each time you go
You leave an empty space inside my heart
Which cannot be filled without you.

I can't make you what you're not
You fear me somehow and have no faith
You need to run, run back to safety
I wouldn't hurt you. I love you so.

Why wouldn't you give me just one chance
A little try, a trial run
Oh no my love not you. You're weak, you think of only you
I know now you have no trust, without that it's no good
I gave you my all, my life, my time and most of all I gave you my love.

The time we have together is mostly happy
I hide the feelings I have when I dread your leaving
When the pain and emptiness will return again
I wanted to share the rest of my life with you my darling
But it was not to be
So I pray that I can love again
To know the love I give, will be returned
Perhaps I may feel again that happy feeling
For longer than one weekend
And spend the rest of my life with my soulmate.

There will always be a special feeling in my heart for you
You are my true friend
My thanks for the good you have done for me.
I must now find a way to break away
The hurt is too bad for me to bear for the rest of my life
Bye, bye my love I'll love and miss you always
Please understand I'll know you'll hurt
Please stand back as I know you will
Whilst I try to build a proper life.

Your woman

Mary L Williamson

YOU AND ME

The house seems so big,
Now there's just you and me.
They've grown and gone,
Soon they will have,
Their own family
It's how it's meant to be,
Just you and me.
But I still love you just the same,
You're my best friend,
It's just the two of us again.

Alison Rainsford

MY MOM

My mom means the world to me
Even though she's gone
And while I cannot see her
In my heart she still lives on.
I had three happy years with her
'Not much,' I hear you say
But she made each second special
In some kind of way
But when she had to go
She made sure I was safe
By phoning Gran and Grandad
To take me to their place
And although the years have passed
I think of her every day
And I know that she is watching me
In her own special way.

Rebecca Leddington

WHEN I FIRST CAME TO THIS LAND

When I first came to this land a paradise it seemed
Fresh green fields as far as the eye could see, no one around
to bother me
Beyond the fields the mountain range and then the sky so brilliant blue

Down near my feet the cool, cool brook trickling over stones,
On its journey with its own purpose
Meandering to where it has to be.

In those days one could drink from this, no thought of pollution here,
No chemicals thrown carelessly on the land, a danger to all that liveth.
No power stations to filthy the air I breathe or factory chimneys either.
We call it progress all the dirt which comes from a car exhaust
Which replace the horse and cart, he'd only need a bale of hay
And he'd give you his heart.

Have we really come so far in these last few thousand years?
The fighting, famine, greed and wars, do not banish all our fears.
Man is the maker of it all and cannot find a way to live in
peace and harmony
And dry up all our tears.

Rosemary Brown

HOW HE MAKES ME FEEL

I run my fingers through your hair
And believe I can walk on air
I gaze into your big blue eyes
And start to float into the sky
Your sweet words
Sound like chirping birds
Your gentle touch
Means so very much
Your sweet smile
Can light up a sundial
All that's left to say really
Is that I love you dearly.

Cheremane Hartery

To Mum

Thank you for understanding me
And showing me you care
For always being good to me
And always being there
Thank you for standing by me
When things have been so bad.
For brightening up my life
Whenever I've been sad.
But there's one more thank you
And I think it's plain to see
That these words come straight
                    from my heart.
Thank you for loving me
Mum I'll love you always.

D D D'eath

REMANATION

Souls of poets dead and gone,
You aery shades attend to me,
Infuse your gifts of poesy
Within my veins, and when it's done
Release the Muses, set them free;
Transmute me to Aganippe,
From far Boeotian Helicon.

Summon forth both Shelly, Keats,
From out of Bardo's abstract plane,
That each may occupy, again,
Their yet unfilled Parnassian seats
Through me, who by their influx gain
New skills, ingrafted to my brain,
That I may duplicate their feats.

Masters of Erato's art,
So tragic, each too young to die;
Our world impoverished thereby,
But transmigration may restart
Your genius, ceded from on high
And thus inbue my soul, that I
Play understudy in your part.

Alasdair Maciver

I NEED MORE THAN A LIFETIME

A lifetime, not enough, I need more
For life comes to the rich and the poor.
God sent me a treasure trove
A Garden of Eden, an orchard grove.

See the freedom of a bird
Hear the softly-spoken word,
A heart so soft to God does plead
With trepidation does precede.

I need more than a lifetime, I need you
For you are all that love does value.
The cost of loving you is great
Endure I must, it's worth the wait.

Denise Shaw

BUTTERFLIES AND SUNSHINE

For eight and a half months he has been in my thoughts,
My heart, my dreams and my head.
His name would drum itself into my mind
At home, at school or in bed.
Since three months ago I have felt his kiss
Like the touch of soft rainfall
His hands have touched me here and there
I felt good about it all.
Recently though his lips touched mine
And it didn't feel the same
I didn't feel the butterflies
I think I'm going insane
There is someone else who makes me feel good
He makes me smile and laugh
To him I talk I don't just speak
I want to follow his path.
So may the lights lead the way
And show us where to go
May the sun come out from behind the clouds
And shine on all below.
Let us all have someone there
To make us feel this way
Problems and joys we can share
Forever and a day.

Fiona McWhirter

TO BE IN LOVE

The greatest feeling in the world,
Is when you are in love.
Although your feet are on the ground,
Your head floats high above.
The bad times in your life,
All fade and disappear.
Though you see the people talking,
Not a single word you hear.
Nothing's too much trouble,
And everything's so grand.
Others think you're not all there
But they don't understand.
You can think of no-one,
But the one that's in your heart,
You're so happy when together,
And so sad when you're apart.
You have a bond between you.
That no-one else can break.
There's something to hold on to,
That no-one else can take.
You're living in a dreamworld,
A world that's all your own
To be in love just has to be,
The finest thing I've known.

S Brown

REQUIEM - (FOR A PARTNER)

What now when someone dear has gone
How can we e'er believe that life goes on.
When all our happiness is in the past
How can we imagine joy will ever last.

What now when days are empty, nights are long
Can we ever find a niche where we belong.
What do we want, what is our yearning now
What brings a smile and smoothes the furrowed brow.

What now when music cannot reach the soul
Do we search for a different goal.
Can we look forward, make another start
Find something yet to ease the aching heart.

What now when all is anguished pain
Is it possible to ever live again.
Can one be strong and wear a radiant smile
Fool everyone around us with our guile.

What now when youth and laughter's far behind
Do we seek solace of a different kind.
A skylark's song, a rose's scent, an infant's cry
Can they sustain us as the years go by.

Do we fight bravely on and win
Determined not to weaken or give in.
Fight the good fight, refuse to yield
Or weaken, be a coward on the field.

The choice is ours to either swim or sink
Once we've been driven to the final brink.
We must be strong and overcome our grief
Look to the future with a strong belief.

Joan Whitehead

A PERFECT WISH

A perfect world
Has drifted away from man's grasp;
It is too far away for any human to reach.
A perfect world would live on love alone,
A place almost unrecognisable in our lives,
Yet familiar to our dreams.

Can there be a world where we truly, sincerely love?
A world where young life is innocent and cherished;
Somewhere we choose to run to, and not from.
To see flowers natural once more; their scent and colour
real to my senses.

Gardens and lands where the trees grow freely,
A world in which fruit remains unaltered by human hand,
Respected for what it is, our sustenance.
A place where our soil is shared freely,
Where there is no time for greed.
All colours standing together as a blanket of comfort,
protecting our earth,
The way it was in the beginning; and the way it should be now.

Christine Nicholson

WAITING

Where does this poet find the source of inspiration?
Where to begin to track such an illusive beast?
How to attempt, through jumbled jungle of wordy consternation
And over high, dry plain to catch the thought on which to feast?

From what illusive marker should I first take my bearing?
And in which pool of direction should I my thoughts immerse?
To decide the bold and worthy cause to which am I declaring
My allegiance and resolve with sword of verse?

The answer is, as yet, still undecided
Proved by page unblemished under writing hand
This train of thoughts unhelpful tracks have yet to guide
Me to some poetically perfect promised land.

But still I shall with patience wait to be enlightened
Transported from dry plains to fields green and lush
That I can know that force within me stirred, aroused and heightened
And feel creation's juices flow with inspiration's rush.

Andy Scott

SANDYMOUNT STRAND

In the furrowed sand,
puddles fill the hollow
spaces where the tide
slowly overtakes the
strollers wandering out
into the vast expanse
of Sandymount Strand.

I recall the time we
sat in the car near
Sligo, tossing Atlantic
waves bamboozling us
and sea circling our
space, the car sinking
in the sliding sand.

Working at our art,
we take risks, move
out into the wider
horizons and flourish
but the surrounding
tide always waiting
to swallow quickly
our masterpieces.

Mary Guckian

TEA WITH A FRIEND

Can I pour you a nice cup of tea?
Strong, with a home made scone
The pot is big and can do for three
But this pleasant day will soon be gone

Help yourself to jam and feel at home
There is some cream as well upon the tray
This is no time to feel alone
We are friends and you are welcome any day

I am a friend in whom you can confide
And a secret you can put into my trust
Nobody can put my loyalty aside
As betrayal shows a moral rust

Come friend! Do not be upset
We may talk through this solution yet.

P Edwards

CASCADE

Cool renaissance lime in a lemon world,
The fountain splutters and spurts in the June light,
Bursting into life as a plethora of drops of water
Fill the gurgling ubiquitous receptacle below,
A storm insinuates itself in the warm air of the afternoon,
Weaving a silken sheet of cloud across the fugitive sun,
Amorphous, shadowy, opaque, the sky is thick with expectation,
Millions of glistening raindrops descend like pearls
Carving rivers and streams on the hard sunbaked earth,
Water flows through the universe, smoothing, polishing, foaming,
Stars shine like diamonds in the wild night sky.

Nigel David Evans

THE MILLENNIUM . . .ONCE UPON A TIME!

Through time and space mankind has travelled . . .
Breaking the barriers of sound -
In far beyonds on planets walking,
Pioneering unknown ground.

Into a galaxy . . . unchallenged,
Uncertain of their destiny -
Mankind searches for salvation . . .
Where time is still eternity.

Time is for ever - without end . . .
But has no resting place . . .
It marches on without a pause . . .
And never alters pace.

Malcolm Wilson Bucknall

FIRST GREAT GRANDCHILD

Soon I'll be a great gran
It should be a joyous day for me
A special day in all of my life
But it just isn't meant to be
Instead it will bring me sorrow
For that little baby I never shall see.
Those little screwed up eyes
That little turned up nose
Those little petted lips
That baby always shows
Those little chubby hands that I shall never hold
It really brings me sorrow
A sorrow so untold
That first little smile I never shall see
Those first words I never shall hear
Those first stumbling steps again I won't see
But altho' I'll never see that baby
He or she is still part of me
Through a simple family fall out
So many years ago
Some of my family I never do see
Altho' I still hold them dear to me
But that's what life is all about
So the love of my family for me
Is something I've learned to do without
To the future mum and dad
To gran and grandad too
My very best wishes go to all of you.

Mary Warnock

GOOD NEWS!

Discharged today - ten years on,
Fate dealt many savage blows
As the shadow hung, unseen!
A mood of gentle optimism has taken root,
But I am wary
The proverbial chickens not yet hatched,
Must wait accountability.
Recollections now:
Remembering how it was, words engraved
In my memory.
Facts and figures, speed essential -
Radiotherapy, behind the mask
The claustrophobic fears of one man.
Four weeks and many prayers,
Then waiting once again.
Sadly the treatment not complete,
Further action - necessary.
The surgeon smiled - reassuringly.
How fortunate to find a bed
At the second attempt,
Intensive care, always in great demand.
And so it was October 1990
Marvellous aftercare!
The love of a good woman, no longer
Here to share the joy.
But offspring who create new life
And give support.
This very day - I thank you all!

T G Bloodworth

AN ODE TO HER

Stroking my unurtured head.
The shallowness of love does not pretend.
She cradles me into her arms instead.
An ode to her is all I can depend.

Her hair is pulled past her ear.
My emptiness fills like water and glass.
An icy heart now soft. Like my fear.
An ode to her is all I can amass.

Colin B Kilday

MY WISH

I'd like to wave a magic wand
and wish for just one thing.
To get rid of all my aches and pains
and be fit again - come spring,
I'd spend more time with others
less fortunate than me,
engage in conversations
and bake them cake for tea.
So until then I'll live in hope
that soon I shall feel well
'Cos there's no such thing as magic -
and only time will tell.

Patricia Whiting

OF THIS KIND

Clever are the poets
Who project ever line
For these descriptive masters
Use blank verse not rhyme
So skilled and crafted
The wordsmith who flows
Though a command in expression
Can rival the prose.

Warren Brown

LOST WISHES

I thought my heart was broken
When she left and went away.
My life was as black as night
And I could not find my way.

But then I met someone else
And at last my life became anew
And this enchanting lady helped me
To keep away all thoughts that were blue.

For when I looked upon her
My heart did skip a beat
And then when she spoke to me
To me it was such a treat.

For I will love her forever
Be it until the end of time.
For even though I knew alas
That she never would be mine.

And when I lay down dying
When I reach the end of my life
My last thoughts will be of her
And how I wished to make her my wife.

B L R Jones

LICKING AT THE TEARS

Coiled around tomorrow
Is a serpent spitting hate
Gently hissing curses
Whilst the hour's growing late.

Fangs that promise death
With sacs of poison to dispense
Throughout the veins of Northern Ireland
Waiting in suspense.

Politics ignores the rattle
Shaking from that tail
And brightly coloured markings
Warn the process dare not fail.

Constricted death comes slowly
And that serpent's jaws gape wide
Licking at its victims' tears
Who scream so, terrified.

Kim Montia

NEXT TIME

I almost won the lottery
that stakes were very high
all that I can do now
is give a great big sigh.

I nearly caught a fish
as big as any pike
but then again I couldn't carry it home
on my rusty old bike.

I almost made the high jump
caught my foot on the post
maybe I would get there
if I didn't always boast.

Hilda Waugh

WHAT IS LOVE?

Is it when you wake up in the morning and
The first thing you see is her face?
You just smile.

Is it the touch of her hand, which makes you
Feel warm inside?

Is it when she smiles it makes you go weak
At the knees?

Is it when she calls out your name, you
Have butterflies in your stomach?

Is it the smell of her hair when you kiss her
Goodbye?

Is it the little things she does which can only
Make you smile?

Is it because you live and breath only for her?

Is it the twinkle in her eye when she says goodbye?
And it feels like forever when she's gone.
Is it when you saw her for the first time you knew
She was the one?
If this is not love
What is love?

Stuart Preece

Looking Out The Window

Bike
Pink tyres
Woman
Bus stop.

House
Lamp post
Car
Red car.

Woman
Fish 'n' chip shop
Garage
Traffic lights.

Zebra crossing
Woman
Bit tits
Little tits.

Big bums
Little bums
Tall women
Small women.

Fat women
Thin women
San Francisco nights
And bus stops.

Paul Boden

SOMETHING SOMEWHERE ELSE

Fish dream of bigger bowls,
Footballers of getting goals.

Cats can catch a mouse
Bigger than a house.

Blank pages, do by stint,
Long for ennobling print.

The chicken for an egg to hatch
The virgin for a perfect match.

All things want change or more:
The rich man to be poor.

The stamp collector thinks a penny black:
Princes of jewels they lack -

The gardener wants to grow a bigger veg
A toppier to cut a stranger hedge.

A stripper to take off more attire:
The arson to make a grander fire.

A baby to be big as dad,
The sorrowful to be made glad.

Thus do women want to be something else
As men are not happy with themselves.

Look around you - all you see:
Dream of what would rather be.

David Hazlett

VICTORY GARDEN

A small pond in the corner of the garden,
A bug eyed frog with brown eyes browsing,
In the sparkling blue pond, with blooming garden,
Blushing golden pears and a white blossom nestle,
Brown speckled, yellow Mexican hat flowers dance,
As a pair of white cranes taking a nip of the cool water,

A charming black mole prepares to enter,
The flower garden with mushrooms and colour,
Blossoms in pink, amethyst and sunflowers tall,
With two mischievous pink pigs peek over a stone,
A stone fence divides the grassy victory garden,
Pink, and white sweet peas climb the stone walls.

A yellow and white spider chrysanthemum opens,
The sunflower blooms on a graceful green stalk,
An intricate root system grasps the ground of hollow,
Sugar peas, Indian squash, tomatoes and a purple eggplant,
Form a dazzling display of nature's bounty in the victory garden,

Rows after rows of carrots and radishes,
The trellis is built high for the climbing vines,
Tulips wave in a light breeze as the bees fly,
Cucumbers and bees early flowers pollinates them,
For the summer when the herbs are pleasant to smell.

Stanley Majors

WEDDING WHISTLE

The balance of sweet dreams,
Fulfils love on perfection
With smiles on horizon
Just two lips beneath the clouds,
Explains truth above love.
It is important to realise the element virtues, are
                              expressed with loving thoughts.

The confidence with an equal solitude,
With selfishness complement, expands to feebleness,
Sweet words are such universe seeming to fulfil, peace of true love.
And to keep loyalties young, with golden passion,
Transcriptions of a dream, have never expressed beauty of liberty.
Although it is important to give the impression of wonderful balance.

Because sweet smiles, gives their own fragrance,
Daily shining, with multitude of a kiss
Expands the pleasure about true happiness,
Marriage is love and trust,
And share each other's pleasure
Which begins on the Wedding Day.

Heather Aspinall

WINTER'S END

We thought it would pass,
The blustering wind and rain,
Give way to sun, at least a blink,
To pierce the scouring clouds refrain.

But no, the breakers curling peaks
Crashed and ground the shore,
Storming winds tossed chimney pots,
Timbers flew and still there was more.

A kind of mayhem perpetual
On the wings of deep Atlantic lows
Bored and battered ceaselessly.
There seemed no end to our woes.

And then it happened at winter's end,
The cloudy wrack split wide in splendour
To show a shaft of sunlight, pale but warm,
Which gently lit the ravaged ground.

And snowdrops, awaiting the sign,
By tree and hedge raised heads white crowned,
Saluting spring at winter's end.

Ellen Worthington

ALL MY CHILDHOOD HEROES

All my childhood heroes
Have grown old, and thoughtful.
I used to watch them,
Sat at home with Dad -
Those rainy days inside
With nothing to do but smile
At how it used to be.
Back then the colours
Were awash with greys,
But the things they did -
With that courage and spirit -
Didn't need a tainted shade.
Everything back then -
Men's minds, and the wives'
Unsung labours -
Everything was so pleasant.
No one mocked the boy in the torn shirt,
Or the girl who couldn't spell
The word *happiness*.
So it's strange now
How that boy and that girl
Are stuck inside a home
Where no one will visit.
And I must ask myself:
Where will I be
When my hero on the sofa
Next to me has forgotten
How it used to be?

Those days of splitting logs,
Or rummaging through the shed
For the blunted axe,
Long since rusted and spent,
Now only faint memories
Of a former life
Of dry eyed days outside.

Rhys Thomas

GOD'S WONDERFUL WORLD

Was it chance that created
The home that we call earth?
Or God's hand and intervention
That gave our world its birth?

Some say it is the selfish gene
That makes the world go round
Our DNA is all that's left
When we are underground.

But others see our planet
As evidence of love
It's stronger than death
And comes from God above.

God's world is all around us
Wonderful and great
If we only take the time to look
Before it is too late!

Margaret Ruscoe

ANTIQUITY

How did I reach this sad state of affairs,
As I sit on my chair,
Once filled with enthusiasm, vigour and
Vim, my mind all alert and my figure all trim,
The wrinkles betray notions dreamt
In my head but my muscles are weak
And my feet are like lead,
I have waltzed and I have done
The twist in step all the same,
Now all I can do is a shuffle with a frame,
I sit here with dozens of wrinklies
Sucking a ginger nut soaked in a cup
Of tea or coffee and a napkin
Adjusted so under my chin to catch
All the bits that my gums
Won't keep in, at night before bed
Sometimes a cuddle would keep
Me all snug up like a bug in a rug.

E Stokes

GREEN AND ECO

There's death in the canals
as they choke with weed
and litter from the street.
Pools of poison . . .
oil slicks blister
the once busy water
where many fish did live and breed.
The barges just rot and decay
like partially submerged ghostly hulks
that were the mainstay
of the area, the arteries
of a busy network.
Too late for tears
as dead fish
and supermarket trollies,
lie side by side
ensnared by overgrown weed,
amidst stagnant sewage
of our own making,
desecration indeed.
But never fear
if we all pay more taxes,
we can clean it all up,
restock it with fish
and fresh oxygenated water,
just as it was
thirty years ago,
now that we are *green* and *eco.*

Ian Mowatt

VIVE LA DIFFÉRENCE!

A friend once told me something,
But I hope he spoke in jest;
He said that girls were simply boys
With dumplings on their chests!

But girls are not the same as boys
(If they are, I'll eat my hat);
In fact, they're very different,
And here's the proof of that:

Boys throw lots of punches
During a boxing match;
But girls never fight like that -
They kick, and bite, and scratch!

Roger Williams

SOMEONE ELSE

I would like another lady
Unlike the one I had before,
Someone to kiss and cuddle
And worship and adore.

Someone to sit and cuddle
And with whom to have a word,
Yes I would like another lady
Not just another bird.

Perhaps we could go for walks
On windy rainy days,
Watch telly in the evening
And get used to each other's ways.

I will show her lots of kindness
How much I care I'd tell her,
Just as long as she never had
A husband or a fella.

But most of them are devious,
I tell by the colour of their eyes,
And all they usually tell me
Is lots and lots of lies.

But after all is said and done
I'm still on me Jack
So I would like a new one
I don't want the others back.

Alex Smith

THE PERFORMANCE

Fiddle fiddling, guitar strumming,
feet and fingers tap,
drinks move in the glass
vibrating to the rhythm.

The mood changes
fiddle becomes violin,
smooth, seductive,
saying things, expressing emotions
that words cannot express.

Songs of love and love lost
of war, protest and politics,
performers work with enviable ease,
but is all what it seems
are they sincere, or
is it well rehearsed professionalism.

Keith R Slatter

MAGIC

There is a place not far from here
Magic beyond belief
Although it's only woods and fields
It brings me such relief.

When I'm unhappy, stressed or sad
I go there right away
And everything which seemed so bad
Is righted while I stay.

Oh come with me and you will see
Exactly what I mean
Doubts and worries disappear
As if they'd never been.

This lovely meadow with its flowers
The woods where sweet birds sing
The hazel which became my bower,
The views, and everything.

For me it's real enchantment here
No witch or magic brew,
But sounds of birdsong, peace and quiet
Tranquillity, rare and true.

Diana Price

DANCE TO YOUR DADDY

'Dance to your daddy
my little lamb.'

Who the daddy?
Who the lamb?

I danced to mine
long years ago
bare feet
on a Chinese carpet
arms flowing
like seaweed
in a rock pool.

Using the age old weapon
to call him
from his world
of red tape
and sealing wax
into my own.

Two of us alone
in that upstairs room
with the lime tree
struggling for life
in the small front garden
with the iron gate.

Deirdre Armes Smith

MY FRIEND'S DOG NAMED LEAKIE

I have a friend with a dog named Leakie
When they come to my home she is very cheeky
She'll come up to me and sit at my feet
It's just that she's asking me for a treat
Then off to the kitchen I go so briskly
To get old Leakie some cheesie biscuits
For these I know she will really enjoy
As she eats them the spittle will run down her jaws
She will look up to me with gleam in her eyes
As to say many thanks for a lovely surprise
Then I'll say come on Leakie and don't be so cheeky
Just lay down and have a sleepy.

Frederick Goff

COMPASSION

Throughout the land, we understand
the promotion of passion,
as children we are taught, stories that please us.
The story and glory of baby Jesus,
we visualise as we realise,
the history of his mystery.
The worth of his time spent on earth,
in our adult, youth, is it not the truth?
Is it the fashion,
to enjoy our sexual ration.
While all of us deplores, conflicts and wars,
for political reasons,
conflicts and wars, are ever in season,
yet at times night and day,
we may display how we feel,
then kneel and pray, as to the Lord we appeal.
For war to cease and bring us peace,
for him to conciliate,
are we then once again,
being too passionate?

Benny Howell

THE AMERICAN DREAM

Giant buildings that reach to the sky
Star studded boulevards, and blueberry pie.
Capital Hill and Madison Square
American dream preached everywhere.
Louder than loud, brighter than bright.
The magic of Disney, what a wonderful sight
Hollywood where stars are born.
Field on field of American Corn the statue
Of Liberty, stands silent and proud, Lincoln
Memorial immersed in a crowd, those special
American things known the world round,
Constitution on which it was found.

But don't be fooled by this gutsy charade
For many Americans, life is unfairly hard.
Decadent decoys hide the real truth.
Of the despair and depravity, that has taken firm.
Root, conveyor belt law not the justice they preach,
Many citizens' rights put far out of sight
Reach, opulence on a scale never seen but
For millions no hope of the American dream,
Proud Indian face, that once scanned the plains,
Scared with the tears of a dying refrain, drugs
And corruption, murder and rape!
Religious fanatics, who would take the juice from grape.

We in Great Britain seem to follow their lead
And some of their bad things in our country breed
Policeman with guns and new baton soon drugs in
Abundance our children to ruin:
American plea bargaining seems on its way,
Our Great Britain, justice
Has seen better days.

Our politicians, who follow their lead creating a
Society based firmly on greed, they can see
The American Dream, as most, already live, in its
Abundant stream, it's time to stop this American
Trend, and for the workers once more to become
Each other's friends we don't need the greed, that politicians
Preach, fight for fairness and equality, for all and
For each other, it's time to share, not hoard away.
It's time to do things the old British way, so
Workers unite as we did long ago, and turn back the
Tide of this American show, replace this
Destructive greed, with everyone's need.

Marion Cornbill

CUPID

It seems we can't choose, who to love,
I couldn't tell you why.
Love doesn't know of religion or race,
When he lets his arrows fly.

Love, will mix ages, colour and creed
There's nothing we can do
But accept our fate with joyful grace
No reason to be blue.

And to those who question such love
There's nothing you can say
Only treat with gentle pity
It may happen to them one day.

Jacqueline Taylor